dwell

Written for
Whitton Avenue Bible Church
2601 E Whitton Avenue
Phoenix, AZ 85016
www.whittonavenue.org

Contents

Introduction

"Chris, I think God wants to break you."

This arrow, let loose by a trusted mentor, pierced my heart with grace and truth. I knew he was right, but not for the reasons you might expect. I had not been caught in a marquee sin nor was I strutting around with pompous arrogance. Yet as he shared observations of my life and public ministry, the Spirit confirmed things I knew to be true. I was not spending enough time with God to be impacted by his holiness and love. I did not live with an awareness of my own deep dependence on God's grace. I was not appropriately affected by the hurts of those around me. As a pastor, my theology may have been fine but my heart needed to be broken.

Brokenness was not a foreign concept to me. More than a decade earlier God began to teach me about it from texts like Isaiah 57:15. "For thus says the One who is high and lifted up, who inhabits eternity, whose name is Holy: 'I dwell in the high and holy place, and also with him who is of a contrite and lowly spirit, to revive the spirit of the lowly, and to revive the heart of the contrite.'" Brokenness is the posture of a heart that is laid low in the presence of God. It is, to use Isaiah's vocabulary, a contrite heart and a lowly spirit. Like its better-known cousins, humility and repentance, brokenness happens when we come to grips with who we are (and are not) in light of who God is.

Brokenness became something I pursued in my relationship with God, a state of heart I sought to maintain. However, like humility and repentance, it is not a default attitude of the human heart. Experiencing brokenness one day does not ensure that it will be there the next. It lies at the bottom of the escalator, yet the stairs always move up, lifting our hearts toward pride and self-sufficiency. Thus the pursuit of brokenness requires intentional movement downward. This is a humbling experience, yet without it we cannot dwell in the breathtaking presence of God.

As I learned from my mentor, the degree to which our hearts are broken before God also affects our interactions with others. Brokenness is a scent, as is pride. These are not as obvious as our words or actions, but they create an atmosphere around us that gives others a sense of how connected we are with our need for God. Our aim in being involved in the lives of others is to point them to Jesus and his power to redeem. But if we do not pursue brokenness, we might find ourselves speaking a gospel about fallen humanity's need for grace while our lives communicate the opposite.

Hearing the words "I think God wants to break you" set me on a journey, a trajectory, but I needed guidance to stay on this trajectory. While God used many human voices to help, the words that ended up giving me the greatest direction were from Jesus' opening teaching in the Sermon on the Mount. We call them beatitudes, from the Latin word for "blessing," because in each beatitude Jesus pronounces a blessing over those who have encountered him. As I meditated, prayed, and preached on these blessings I discovered the trajectory of brokenness. It begins with someone who embraces his or her spiritual bankruptcy and ends with that same person so invigorated by God's agenda to make all things right that he or she will endure persecution with joy. To use the language of Isaiah 57:15, God revives the heart of the contrite.

More than anything, Jesus' blessings give me permission to come to him when I find myself again confronted with remaining sin in my life. The progression from "poor in spirit" to "persecuted" is an ongoing trajectory, not a one-time fix. So when more rebellion and impurity surfaces in my heart–even in the midst of showing mercy or pursuing peace–I must go back to square one to confess my poverty of spirit before God and get back on the trajectory of brokenness.

It was during such a time of coming to Jesus with my spiritual bankruptcy that I sensed God's leading to put this experience together in a way that others could walk through it as well. The aim of this devotional is to familiarize you with the trajectory of brokenness, explore how this plays out in ministry to others, and delight in the blessings Jesus promises. Each devotion includes my reflections on one beatitude, followed by questions to work through. Do not rush through these. Allow the questions to peel back layers of your heart that need to be explored. Write, write, write as much as you can about what you are experiencing, whether in the space provided or in a separate journal. Go beyond the questions to write about other issues the reading stirs up in your heart. If you need further help to understand the beatitude or to guide your processing, I have included scriptures for deeper exploration.

This will be most effective when done in community, whether with your spouse or in a same-gender small group (3-5) or one-on-one setting. The devotions are designed to be between you and God, but the experience of brokenness will be much deeper when you share with others what God is showing you from his word and about yourself. Plus, you can build accountability into your life when at least one other person knows the areas where you need to repent most frequently.

Your journey will begin the same place mine did, with someone saying to you, "I think God wants to break you." So I say that to you now: I think God wants to break you. I say it because I know God wants to spread the fragrance of Christ through your life. I say it because hurting people around you need to see what it looks like to receive God's grace daily. I say it not because you have never tasted brokenness but because you wake up every morning with a fresh need to grow deeper in humility. I say it because brokenness is the trajectory of life that will bring you the deepest intimacy with God and others, a path full of significance, purpose, redemption, joy, and hope. I say it because God's power, love, and faithfulness are most on display when your heart is most dependent on him.

I pray you will join me in this trajectory of brokenness, and do so with trusted friends in Christ. You can take the first step by writing down answers to the questions below.

❖Brokenness is the posture of a heart that is laid low in the presence of God. When have you experienced brokenness in your life? Were they one-time events or seasons?

❖Describe your experience of brokenness currently.

❖What fears or doubts or other expectations do you have about intentionally pursuing brokenness?

Part I

Dwell With Jesus
Until You Are Broken

1: Introduction

"Blessed are the poor in spirit, for theirs is the kingdom of heaven.

Blessed are those who mourn, for they shall be comforted.

Blessed are the meek, for they shall inherit the earth.

Blessed are those who hunger and thirst for righteousness, for they shall be satisfied" (Matthew 5:3–6).

When I was in the "just friends" relationship stage with my wife, I faced a quandary. I knew Rachael well enough to have great admiration for her intellect, her dependability, and her deep relationship with God. But I knew many such young ladies and, like Rachael, they all lived hundreds of miles away. How would I know if she were "the one"? How would I know if I should pursue her?

Into this confusion shone a light from that one human source so many confused men rely upon: Mama. After I rambled my way through the intellectual and philosophical considerations of this situation to my Mama, she spoke this piece of wisdom into my life–"You will never know if you love her if you are not around her."

As is usually the case, it turns out that Mama was right. Not long after our conversation, Rachael and I realized we were passing through the same city on the same day and the rest is history. We planned dinner and within about four minutes of sitting across the table from Rachael, I experienced not only an intellectual and spiritual admiration for her, I felt new affections for her. In her presence I experienced something entirely new and my life would never be the same.

In the opening words of the Sermon on the Mount, Jesus pronounces blessings over the poor in spirit, mournful, meek, and hungry and thirsty for righteousness (Matthew 5:3-6). We might hear in this teaching a divine preference for those who are, by nature, prone to melancholy and self-deprecation. But Jesus is not blessing a particular emotional disposition. Neither is Jesus commanding us to make ourselves poor in spirit, mournful, meek, or hungry and thirsty for righteousness. Rather, he is declaring blessings on us if we experience these postures of the heart when we encounter him. Like my life-changing encounter with Rachael, these blessed affections arise not from intellectual consideration or logical conclusions but from being changed in the presence of Jesus.

This is what the apostle Peter experienced one morning after a long, futile night of fishing. Jesus—a carpenter, not a fisherman—climbed into Peter's boat and told him to lower the nets one last time. When Peter complied, the same nets that had surfaced empty time after time were now breaking from the huge catch. Peter was no genius but he knew fishing well enough to realize that those fish were overloading his nets because Jesus commanded them to. In the face of such unrivaled authority, Peter "fell down at Jesus' knees, saying, 'Depart from me, for I am a sinful man, O Lord'" (Luke 5:8).

The beauty of Jesus is that he refuses to depart from us in these moments of conviction. Rather than being disgusted by our exposed brokenness and moving on to more "put-together" people, he stays. In fact, he does more than stay. When we embrace our brokenness before him, Jesus blesses us. He grants us favor for coming to terms with the reality of who he is and who we are. That process of experiencing brokenness in the presence of Jesus is what we will explore in the first four beatitudes.

Of course, we do not have the privilege of Jesus stepping into our fishing boat and flexing his divine muscles. Our encounter with Jesus is not in the flesh, but in the record of his life in the flesh throughout the pages of the gospels. Yet as we read of Jesus' miraculous birth, his faithful obedience to his Father, his displays of compassion, his mighty deeds, and his death and resurrection for sinners, the Spirit can take us into the same potent presence that Peter experienced. There, where our sinful hearts are fully exposed, we have the opportunity to be broken, confess who we really are, and begin the process of transformation.

Thus, if we are to dwell with Jesus until we are broken, we must commit daily and other extended times to commune with Christ through prayer, meditating on his word, and writing out what God is doing in our hearts. There is simply no substitute for undistracted, focused time if we are to experience the types of encounters we read about in the Scriptures.

Yet there is another factor to this process, one that we cannot schedule. God is often pleased to move us along the trajectory of brokenness by trials that lie outside of our control: the fractured relationship, the terminally-ill friend, the financial burden, the frustrating job situation. Rather than going down the path of bitterness, cynicism, and despair, God can lead us down the path of humility, grieving, and relinquishment. We may not be able to change the situation but we can allow God to change us through it.

As I have stood at this fork in the road many times, one story that has encouraged me toward brokenness is from the life of William Carey, the father of the modern Protestant missions movement. Carey's pioneering labors in India included the development of dictionaries, grammar books, and translations of the Bible into local languages so God's written word could spread. This was long, arduous work. Then the unthinkable happened. On March 11, 1812, a fire destroyed nearly 20 years' worth of this linguistic labor. All the books and printing presses were reduced to ashes. There was no flash drive or cloud support to backup the work. In one night, two decades of toil went up in flames.

Carey was told the news by a close friend, and his eyes immediately filled with tears. Later as he processed the event, he reflected that perhaps there was too much "self-congratulation" in his missionary endeavor. Then he said, "The Lord has laid me low, that I may look more simply to him."[1]

This is the type of response to trials and posture of brokenness I yearn to have. I pray our journey through the beatitudes helps you in nurturing such a heart as well.

Questions for reflection

❖Have you encountered Jesus in a way that made you want to say "Depart from me"? Describe the encounter and your response.

―――――――――

[1] Mary Drewry, *William Carey: A Biography*, p. 154
    http://www.desiringgod.org/resource-library/sermons/the-lord-stood-by-me-that-all-the-nations-might-hear

❖As one who has already trusted in Christ for salvation, what do you feel when you bring your sin and deficiencies into his presence?

❖Spending time in Jesus' presence requires intentionality. My recommendation is that, apart from daily times of communion with God, you should have at least one weekly hour of solitude where you can be in the presence of Jesus with open Bible, open heart, and open journal to process through God's work in your life. Pray about what type of time commitment God wants you to make during the course of walking through this devotional and write down your commitment below.

2: Blessed are the poor in spirit

We do not naturally embrace the status of "poor." For starters, it carries a negative connotation we understandably avoid, and beyond that, we can always point to someone who has fewer resources than we do. I will never forget interacting with children in rural Appalachia who had no idea that they were, by American standards, poor. Compared to the upper-middle class community I grew up in, they had nothing. Yet they knew people deeper in the mountain hollers with even less, so they had no reason to accept a negative label. One grandmother in that context talked to me about growing up in the Great Depression, when everyone was poor. Her mother used to tell her, "We may be poor, but at least we're not dirty!"

Such is our tendency to assume the best about ourselves. In terms of physical wealth, this can be a great thing if it nurtures contentment. But if your heart says, "...at least I'm not ____" about your spiritual condition, you have located the place where the trajectory of brokenness must begin.

Jesus pronounces blessings first on those who are poor in spirit. One Bible commentator writes that the best synonym for "poor in spirit" is "desperate." He explains, "'The poor in spirit' are ultimately those standing without pretense before God, stripped of all self-sufficiency, self-security, and self-righteousness."[2] Another author writes, "The 'poor' in the Old Testament is one who is both afflicted and unable to save himself, and who therefore looks to God for salvation, while recognizing that he has no claim upon him... To be 'poor in spirit' is to acknowledge our spiritual poverty, indeed our spiritual bankruptcy before God."[3]

---

[2] Robert Guelich, *The Sermon on the Mount*, p. 98

[3] John Stott, *The Message of the Sermon on the Mount*, pp. 38-39

We often militate against such acknowledgments. If you are like me, you keep one eye on your moral respectability and one eye on those with less of it than you. With such a focus, it can be easy to maintain an air of decency. And it is precisely that focus that must change if we are to come to terms with our poverty of spirit. The key phrase in both of the quotes above is "before God." We do not experience poverty of spirit before others because we are not spiritually poor compared to them. We experience spiritual poverty in the presence of God where we behold his spiritual wealth and have our poverty exposed.

This thread runs throughout the biblical story. In the presence of God, Adam and Eve knew themselves to be guilty of eating the forbidden fruit (Genesis 3). In the presence of God, Abraham fell on his face (Genesis 17). In the presence of God in the burning bush, Moses knew himself to be inadequate for the task of delivering God's people (Exodus 3-4). In the presence of God, Isaiah saw his sin and cried out, "Woe is me! For I am lost; for I am a man of unclean lips, and I dwell in the midst of a people of unclean lips; for my eyes have seen the King, the LORD of hosts!" (Isaiah 6:5) In the presence of God the Son, the risen Jesus, Saul of Tarsus was knocked to the ground, blinded, and convicted of his sins against Jesus' followers (Acts 9).

Thus the banner over these first four beatitudes is to "dwell with Jesus until you are broken." The idea is not that you are spiritually whole and need breaking but that your spiritual brokenness will not be unveiled unless you encounter Jesus in all of his splendor. This was my experience in the story I shared earlier. The root of my lack of brokenness was not that I was spiritually flawless; rather, I was keeping my distance from God's holy presence so my deficiencies were not being exposed.

Brokenness is a journey that requires boldness. You must be willing to confront some unsavory things about your heart as you allow God to expose your true motives with the light of his holiness. It would be much easier to adopt a "Don't ask, don't tell" policy about what really lies underneath your words and actions. Because you trust in Jesus for salvation you may reason that there is no need to dig any deeper in your interior life.

With this in mind, let me offer you words of reassurance and incentive as you enter into this trajectory of brokenness. First, let me reassure you that, if you have repented of your sins and trusted in Jesus' death and resurrection on your behalf, you have nothing to lose in this venture. Nothing in your heart that will be unveiled in the holy presence of God will be surprising to him. Those sinful patterns and idolatries have already put Jesus to death in your place. Because of Christ's work for you, brokenness can happen in a context of abundant grace. God loves you and is committed to your holiness. He is eternally faithful to his covenant with you. Entering into a life of brokenness may be painful but it will be for your ultimate good.

If that is the reassurance, what is the incentive? In short, brokenness will deepen your intimacy with God. This is a great paradox—the very presence of God that exposes your spiritual poverty will become your greatest treasure. God's presence is the only place in the universe where there is "fullness of joy" and "pleasures forevermore" (Psalm 16:11). In his presence there is an abundant feast and a river of delights (Psalm 36:8). It is a place of safety, security, and refuge. It is the only place where you will forever belong. Yet, as we have already seen, there is only one type of person who dwells with God in his holy presence: "him who is of a contrite and lowly spirit" (Isaiah 57:15). Or, as Isaiah 66:2 puts it, the God who made all things and needs nothing takes note of only one posture of heart: "he who is humble and contrite in spirit and trembles at my word."

In the presence of God you must either embrace the reality of who you are or run away from him. There is no hiding, no pretense under his all-seeing eye. Yet when you confess that you are poor in spirit, you can experience the incomparable blessing of communion with him. I pray this incentive of deepening nearness to our glorious God emboldens you to take a deep breath and enter into the trajectory of brokenness.

Questions for reflection

❖What do you point to when you want to impress others (family, education, accomplishment, connections, wealth, spiritual devotion, etc.)?

❖Do you bring that confidence into your relationship with God, believing these strong points should impress him as well?

❖What situations reveal your weakness the most?

❖How do you respond to these situations? Do you avoid, ignore, dismiss, or rage against what they reveal, or do you allow them to drive you to the presence of Jesus and embrace your poverty?

❖The Bible affirms both that humans are created in God's image, with dignity and purpose, and that our sinful rebellion has left us unable to live out that identity apart from redemption in Christ. Which unhealthy end of the spectrum do you tend toward: feeling worthless with no chance of change or denying how spiritually bankrupt you are?

❖What is more difficult for you to feel: that you are blessed if you are poor in spirit or that you must embrace your poverty of spirit to experience Jesus' blessing?

Scriptures for deeper exploration

❖Encounters with God's holiness that exposed spiritual poverty:
- Job 38-42
- Isaiah 6
- Mark 4:35-41
- Revelation 1:9-20

❖Psalms expressing desperation for God:
- Psalm 40
- Psalm 70
- Psalm 86
- Psalm 109

❖Examples of believers in touch with their spiritual poverty:
- Exodus 3
- 2 Samuel 7
- Daniel 2:1-30
- 1 Timothy 1:12-17

3: Blessed are those who mourn

Filmmaker and atheist Woody Allen has never been shy about vocalizing his bleak outlook on the world and our life in it. In a radio interview, he shared that he makes films because all the work of shooting and editing distracts him from "the real agonies of the world" such as "the uncertainty of life, the inevitability of aging and death, death of loved ones, mass killings, starvations, holocausts, and… [my conclusion that life] is just a random, meaningless event."

Allen goes on, "These are pretty depressing thoughts, and if you spend much time thinking about them, you can't resolve them—you sit frozen in your seat; you can't even get up to have your lunch. So it's better to distract yourself, and people distract themselves creatively in the arts, they distract themselves in business or by following baseball teams and worrying over batting averages and who wins the pennant. These are all things that you do and focus on rather than sit at home and worry."[4]

There are only two options for addressing reality in Allen's view: despair or distraction. However, when Jesus says "blessed are those who mourn," he calls us to face the "real agonies of the world" head on in a third way, by grieving. Unlike despair, mourning and grief acknowledge not only that misery exists but also—against Woody Allen's worldview—that these exist because something has been lost. God's good creation has been fractured and the one preaching the Sermon on the Mount has come to restore what has been broken. Jesus would bear the real agonies of the world on his own shoulders until they killed him. He died so that sorrow might be undone and harmony with God and one another renewed.

---

[4] From Allen's June 15, 2009 interview on Fresh Air. http://www.npr.org/templates/story/story.php?storyId=105400872

Jesus' call for us to engage our broken world through mourning begins at the personal level. James, Jesus' half-brother, unpacked what this looks like in the fourth chapter of his letter. He noted the quarrels and fighting amongst God's people–the social problem–then traced the problem down to individual greed and discontent. Rather than masking these sinful postures with distraction or leaving his readers to despair, James commanded them to mourn. "Draw near to God, and he will draw near to you. Cleanse your hands, you sinners, and purify your hearts, you double-minded. Be wretched and mourn and weep. Let your laughter be turned to mourning and your joy to gloom. Humble yourselves before the Lord, and he will exalt you" (James 4:8–10).

Mourning starts with our own sin, as we take stock of the damage our rebellion and self-centeredness has created. Mourning is the experience of looking at the brokenness within and around us and asking, "What have I done?! What have we done?!" While the fallout of our ways manifests socially in broken families, injustice against the powerless, wars, and genocide, the cross of Christ remains the most poignant and personal display of the consequence of human sin. There I am reminded that I have ignored my glorious Creator, trespassed his law, used people for my selfish desires, and perpetuated injustice. Under the judgment of a holy God, only the bloody, beaten, suffocating Jesus adequately displays the punishment my sin deserves. As much as watching the news should bring me to tears over the fractured state of God's good creation, the cross is where the deepest divine and human mourning takes place.

This was articulated by Saint Augustine who imagined himself beholding, in person, Jesus suffering on the cross. These are Augustine's meditations on the reason for Jesus' sufferings.

What have you done, oh sweetest child,
that you should be judged so,
oh loving youth, that you should be brought to this?

What is your offense, what is your crime,
what is the cause of your death,
what is the reason for your condemnation?

I am the blow which brings you pain
I am at fault that you are murdered
I am to blame for your death
and for the shame of your punishment
I, I am the bruise of your agony,
the hardship of your torment

I indeed acted wickedly, you were chastised in retribution
I committed the deed, you were beaten in punishment
I exalted myself, you were humiliated
I was full of pride, you were humbled
I took what was forbidden,
you suffered the sharpness of death
I tasted the sweetness of the fruit,
yours was the bitterness of gall.[5]

Though such meditations may strike us as morbid or morose in the short term, they deal with the reality of our hearts and our world that most people ignore. If we are to experience greater depths of dwelling with Jesus, we must learn to grieve over the sin within us and the effects of sin around us. As we begin at the cross, we taste not only the bitterness of our sin but the freedom and joy that come from the forgiveness Christ has made possible.

---

[5] From The Meditations of St. Augustine, used in the Passion Motets of Heinrich Schütz, SWV 56-60

Questions for reflection

❖ At times we need to mourn not only over our particular sin but where that sin can lead (i.e., lust leads to sexual violence, hate leads to murder, greed leads to stealing). What are the results or possibilities of your sinful patterns that you need to mourn over?

❖ True mourning over sin takes place at the cross, where we see Christ–the sinless, righteous one–suffering and dying for our sins. Think of the last time you confessed sin to God. Did this include dwelling before the crucified Jesus and feeling the weight of your sin? If not, how would that make your experience of repentance different?

❖We also experience God's forgiveness because of Jesus' death for us. Are you more likely to skip the mourning and jump straight to forgiveness or do you mourn to the neglect of receiving forgiveness? How can you meditate on Christ's death for you in a fuller way that both mourns and tastes the joy of being forgiven?

❖When faced with the "real agonies of the world," are you more prone to fall into distraction or despair? What does this look like for you?

Scriptures for deeper exploration

❖Prayers of confession or grief over sin:
- Psalm 6
- Psalm 32
- Psalm 38
- Psalm 51
- Psalm 102
- Psalm 130
- Psalm 143

❖Examples of biblical mourning (whether personal or communal sin):
- Ezra 9
- Nehemiah 1
- Lamentations
- Daniel 9:1-23
- James 4:1-10

4: Blessed are the meek

I am no golfer, nor do I aspire to be, but I have always been fascinated by one of the core maxims of golf instructors: "Let the club do the work." As counter-intuitive as it may seem, the first priority of the golfer is not to crush the ball as hard as possible, but to swing the club with the technique that will maximize the club's impact on the ball. I have heard some golfers note that their longest drives down the fairway came after shoulder injuries that forced them to focus on technique rather than power. The club did the work.

Such is the paradox of meekness. In short, meekness is letting the club do the work. I relinquish my agenda for God's agenda. I choose to trust rather than to assert my self-centered desire. Meekness is not inactivity–we still have to swing the club–but an active rest in God's power to accomplish his good purposes.

Jesus' pronouncement of blessing over the meek borrows from one of Israel's corporate songs, Psalm 37. This Psalm is an extended exhortation to those who are oppressed by powerful, corrupt people who ruthlessly take what they want. In such situations the first instinct is to fight back. Yet the writer of the song calls God's people–the righteous poor–to a different tack with these commands:

Fret not yourself because of evildoers...
Trust in the LORD and do good...
Commit your way to the LORD;
Trust in him, and he will act...
Be still before the LORD and wait patiently for him;
Fret not yourself over the one who prospers in his way...
Refrain from anger, and forsake wrath!

In just a little while, the wicked will be no more;
though you look carefully at his place, he will not be there.
But the meek shall inherit the land
and delight themselves in abundant peace.
(Psalm 37:1, 3, 5, 7-8, 10-11)

This song calls God's people to trust, to refrain from anger, to be still, and not to fret (or give in to worry and anxiety). This is the very opposite of what our fear and adrenaline tell us to do. But for Israel, there was a good reason to embrace the meek approach: God had promised the land to his people and would be faithful to act on that promise. His people's role was to rest in his ability to perform what he had promised.

Ancient Israel's crossroads regarding the land serves as a cautionary tale for our walk of faith today. In the letter to the Hebrews, the author recounts Israel's initial failure to enter into the Promised Land following the exodus from Egypt, noting that "they were unable to enter because of unbelief" (Hebrews 3:19). In the language of Psalm 37, they allowed themselves to fret because of evildoers and refused to trust in the LORD and allow him to act on their behalf. The author of Hebrews warns his readers not to fall into the same unbelief with this call to meekness: "Let us therefore strive to enter that rest, so that no one may fall by the same sort of disobedience" (Hebrews 4:11).

Opportunities abound in daily life for us to practice meekness, to strive to rest. There is only so much we can do to keep enough business coming in to keep the company afloat. Our bodies will only heal so fast. We can put parameters on our children's behavior but cannot change their hearts. The dream job remains either elusive or unprofitable. The counseling and medicine are not addressing the emotional disposition that plagues us. Our sinful desires keep us in cycles of struggle.

Circumstances like these bring us to a decision point where we can choose fretting, anger, or meekness, and we take the first step onto the path of meekness through prayer. Prayer is active rest; it is bold relinquishment. When we pray as Jesus teaches later in the Sermon on the Mount, we release our agenda for God's agenda: "Hallowed be your name [that is, may your name be revered as holy]. Your kingdom come, your will be done, on earth as it is in heaven" (Matthew 6:9–10). We center our hearts on his purposes and submit all our fretful worries to his priorities.

When we pray from this place of meekness, we can pray confidently that God will meet our holistic daily needs–the physical ("Give us this day our daily bread"), relational ("forgive us our debts, as we also have forgiven our debtors"), and spiritual ("lead us not into temptation, but deliver us from evil"). Rather than allowing these needs to work us into fretting or anger, we tap into God's own passion to display his greatness. Such a connection comes through rest and relinquishment yet energizes us for prayer and trust and obedience in a way no human motivation could.

This prayerful path is the same we first walked at conversion. Meekness is embedded in our response of faith to the gospel when we release our control over our lives, receive Christ's forgiveness, and confess that Jesus is Lord. Until Jesus returns we must walk this road of submitting our self-centered agenda to God's God-centered agenda. As we will see in part 3, the beautiful paradox of this road is where it leads–"the meek shall inherit the earth." The end of the path of meekness shines brightly with the promise of a resurrected earth that will belong wholly to those who have submitted to God rather than clawing after their piece of land in this life.

Questions for reflection

❖What is meekness?

❖What are the circumstances that stir up fretting, anger, and impatience in you? What does your sinful response look like in these situations?

❖What would it look like for you to experience stillness, trust, patience, and relinquishment in these situations?

❖In your prayer life, what steps can you take to center your heart more on God's agenda?

Scriptures for deeper exploration

❖Biblical characters who modeled meekness during intense trials:
  • Joseph (Genesis 37-50)
  • Moses (Numbers 12)
  • David (1 Samuel 16-31)
  • Daniel and friends (Daniel 1-3, 6)
❖Jesus' example of submission to his Father's agenda:
  • Matthew 26:36-46
  • John 5:18-47
  • John 7:14-18

5: Blessed are those who hunger and thirst for righteousness

The aim of this devotional thus far has been for you to allow Jesus to expose your spiritual brokenness and deep need for him. This process digs down to the core of who you are and thus has very personal consequence. But the beauty of this deep work God does in you is that he transforms you in those deep places. Acknowledging your spiritual poverty, mourning over your sin, and relinquishing control of your life to God positions you to experience the renewal of your desires. This is the natural flow of brokenness, as God communicates in Isaiah 57:15–"to revive the spirit of the lowly, and to revive the heart of the contrite."

This renewal reaches its fullest expression in Jesus' fourth blessing: "Blessed are those who hunger and thirst for righteousness." Here Jesus employs the language of appetite to identify what transformed desires look like, that is, how we know when we are moving from spiritual sickness into spiritual health. When we first come to Jesus, we come with self-centered cravings that leave very little desire for God. This is part of our spiritual poverty that we confess. However, our encounter with Jesus changes us in such a way that our hunger and thirst shifts; we now have an appetite for righteousness.

What exactly do we crave when we hunger and thirst for righteousness? Righteousness is a biblical concept with great width and depth, yet it can be summarized simply: righteousness is right relationships with God and others. It all started in the Garden of Eden, where Adam and Eve enjoyed perfect, unsullied, harmonious relationships with God and one another. They were naked and unashamed–perfect relational intimacy–and they walked with God in the cool of the day. All was well. Righteousness was the reality.

Sin brought this reality to a tragic demise. Adam and Eve's rejection of God as their King not only caused them to hide from their Creator, it turned them against each other. These individual relational fractures in Genesis 3 became institutionalized as people, exiled from Eden, built cities and developed cultures. By the time of the building of the Tower of Babel in Genesis 11, humans had woven their rebellion against God into the very fabric of their society. In short, righteousness was absent at every level of human interaction—with God, with one another, and in the systems and structures of civilization.

In this beatitude, therefore, Jesus is blessing those who recognize this absence of righteousness and crave its restoration. He pronounces favor over those who hunger and thirst for things to be right again at every level. To use more familiar terms, this involves both evangelism (calling people to a right relationship with God through Christ) and social justice (laboring toward right relationships with one another). The second, horizontal aspect of righteousness is detailed more in the second set of beatitudes, so we will address that in the next part and focus here on right relationship with God.

Hungering and thirsting for right relationship with God is craving after God himself. This was expressed by King David, who used his experience of hunger in the wilderness to articulate his heart after God:

O God, you are my God; earnestly I seek you;
my soul thirsts for you; my flesh faints for you,
as in a dry and weary land where there is no water.
So I have looked upon you in the sanctuary,
beholding your power and glory.
Because your steadfast love is better than life,
my lips will praise you.
So I will bless you as long as I live;
in your name I will lift up my hands.

My soul will be satisfied as with fat and rich food,
and my mouth will praise you with joyful lips.
(Psalm 63:1–5)

With David's words in mind, look back over your journey into brokenness thus far and consider the transformation you have experienced by dwelling with Jesus. You enter into God's presence spiritually poor and, by the power of the Spirit, can be changed into one whose heart says, "earnestly I seek you" and "your steadfast love is better than life." This is the intimacy with God that brokenness creates. Though difficult and costly, the path of confessing our poverty, mourning over our sin, and relinquishing control of our lives leads to this glorious place of delight in God himself.

This transformation would not be possible apart from Jesus' reconciling death and resurrection. At the cross he sacrificed his own right relationship with his Father and took on the relational separation we deserved because of our sin. Brokenness returns us to our initial posture at conversion, where we realized that we could never make things right with God through our own efforts and instead received this righteousness through Jesus. As we will see in the days ahead, the repentance and trust we first confessed at conversion remain our ongoing experience that moves us along the trajectory of brokenness.

Questions for reflection

❖What does your heart often hunger and thirst after more than God?

❖What sinful desires do you need to confess before God (this is a specific way to acknowledge your poverty of spirit)? What righteous desires do you want to experience?

❖Describe a time when you had a greater hunger and thirst for God than you do now.

❖ What practical steps do you need to take to nurture a deeper craving for God? Possible answers could include accountability with trusted friends over sinful longings, more meditation on God in his word, cutting out distracting factors like media or entertainment, and longer seasons of communion with God through prayer, silence, and solitude.

Scriptures for deeper exploration

❖ Biblical characters who modeled hunger and thirst after God himself:
- Faithful Israelites (Hebrews 11:1-12:2)
- Jesus (Luke 4:1-13, John 4:31-38, Matthew 26:36-46)
- Paul (Philippians 3)
- Saints in Heaven (Revelation 7:13-17)

❖ Psalms expressing a craving after God:
- Psalm 26
- Psalm 27
- Psalm 36
- Psalm 42
- Psalm 63
- Psalm 84

Part II

Dwell With The Broken
Until They See Jesus

6: Introduction

"Blessed are the merciful, for they shall receive mercy.
Blessed are the pure in heart, for they shall see God.
Blessed are the peacemakers, for they shall be called sons of
God.
Blessed are those who are persecuted for righteousness' sake, for
theirs is the kingdom of heaven" (Matthew 5:7–10).

Since 1843, when Charles Dickens introduced him to the English-speaking world, Ebenezer Scrooge has symbolized both miserliness and the possibility of individual transformation. At the beginning of *A Christmas Carol*, Dickens describes Scrooge's lack of compassion from the inside out: "The cold within him froze his old features, nipped his pointed nose, made his eyes red, his thin lips blue, and he spoke out shrewdly in his grating voice." Thanks to dreams of visitations by the ghosts of Christmas past, present, and future, Ebenezer Scrooge was able to see himself for what he really was—a man so destructively self-consumed that only his death would bring comfort to others. In his dream he beheld grave robbers plundering his fortune and came to terms with the meaningless of a life not lived for the good of those around him.

From these visions Scrooge awakened a new man. He danced around his room and laughed for the first time in years. He anonymously sent a great Christmas turkey to his needy employee's family, pledged a generous donation to charity, and walked about the town, greeting neighbors and patting children on the head. In short, Ebenezer Scrooge experienced transformation with a purpose. His repentance from heartless greed necessarily translated into generosity toward the needy. He went to bed "a squeezing, wrenching, grasping, scraping, clutching, covetous old sinner" who saw the poor as "the surplus population" he would like to see decreased, and because of his encounter with the Christmas ghosts, awoke a laughing, open-hearted model of generosity.

The process of brokenness described in Jesus' first four blessings (Matthew 5:3-6) is transformation with a purpose. Jesus takes spiritually bankrupt sinners like us, welcomes us into his presence, and by the power of his Spirit, brings about a spiritual metamorphosis. Like Scrooge's dreams of the three ghosts, our encounter with King Jesus changes our hearts that only beat for sinful cravings into hearts that beat for God's rule and blessing to be experienced by others.

We have seen that Jesus' first four beatitudes describe how the Spirit fills our spiritually empty lives with righteous longings. The second set of four blessings describes the outworking of those righteous longings into the pursuit of mercy and justice for those around us. Thus, while the banner over the first four is "Dwell with Jesus until you are broken," the banner of the second four is "Dwell with the broken until they see Jesus."

The call to dwell with the broken until they see Jesus is built into the mercy, peacemaking, and pursuit of righteousness taught in Matthew 5:7-8, 10. But Jesus reinforces this even more explicitly in the next section, the pronouncement that his followers are the "salt of the earth" and the "light of the world" (Matthew 5:13-14). Both salt and light have two crucial qualities that make them useful: they are simultaneously distinct from and immersed in the place they are needed. Without both they are not useful. Jesus highlights the need for salt to be distinct with his warning about salt that has "lost its taste." It can be rubbed into meat–immersed where it is needed–but if it is not distinct then "it is no longer good for anything" (Matthew 5:13). Then Jesus highlights the need for light to be immersed where it is needed. The fact that light is distinct from darkness is obvious, but if it is not dwelling where it is needed, or hidden under a basket, then it is of no use. Distinct and immersed. (We will look more at this in the section on "Blessed are the pure in heart.")

Thus when Jesus pronounces, "You are the salt of the earth… You are the light of the world" (Matthew 5:13-14), he is calling us to immerse ourselves in the lives of others and remain distinct from them. He desires for us to both walk in righteous ways and dwell with the broken. This is no easy task. We are pliable folk who are as prone to peer pressure now as when we were younger. So when we spend enough time in someone's life to actually make a difference, we open ourselves up to being affected negatively. This threatens our "saltiness," our Christlike distinction. Yet we must not retreat from the messy lives of others in some attempt to avoid this influence. If you have encountered anything so far in this study, hopefully it has been the messiness of your own life in the holy presence of God. Jesus moved toward you in that needy state and calls you to do the same. The spiritually broken people in your circles may be in line at a soup kitchen, behind the mahogany desk in the corporate office, or tugging at your arm for more breakfast. Whoever they are, Jesus' transforming power in your life is meant to be shared with them.

As challenging as it may be to be simultaneously distinct from and immersed in the lives of hurting people, this is the heart of our mission. Jesus communicated the aim of this mission of being salt and light with the command, "let your light shine before others, so that they may see your good works and give glory to your Father who is in heaven" (Matthew 5:16). This could have easily been Jesus' own mission statement. He is the light of the world (John 8:12, 9:5) and the purpose of his light–his good works of healing, deliverance, compassion, reconciliation, and sacrifice–was to display the glory of his Father. Yet he did not accomplish this like a superhero swooping in to save the day. He lingered in conversation with those in need, moved toward those outcast by society, and ate meals with sinners. That is, he dwelled with the broken. In that context of sharing time, life, and food, his Father's glory was on display.

If you take Jesus' call to this type of ministry seriously, you should be overwhelmed by now. You know yourself, the weakness of your heart, and what struggles could be exposed by distinct-and-immersed ministry to broken people. I have good news for you. The impure motives and sinful inclinations that will inevitably emerge in ministry are simply new evidences of your spiritual poverty and thus new opportunities to experience the trajectory of brokenness. My own experience is that many of my issues of impatience, love of praise, and selfishness did not surface until I moved more intentionally into the lives of others. Ministry may not make us more sinful, but it will expose more of our sin. Furthermore, our ongoing experiences of brokenness and renewal in the presence of Jesus can serve as real-life examples of gospel transformation to those we serve. When we speak truthfully both about Jesus and our own lives, we teach and model his power to change broken sinners.

This second part will walk through the second set of beatitudes that describe salt-and-light, distinct-and-immersed ministry. This will only be helpful to the degree that you apply it to your life, so answer the following questions and open your heart to the transformative work Jesus will do both in you and through you.

Questions for reflection

❖ Using your own words, describe the type of ministry Jesus calls us to when he says that we are the salt of the earth and light of the world.

❖ As you consider your relationships with people in your home, neighborhood, workplace, classroom, or other circles, who are the 3 people God has called you to minister to the most?

❖ What challenges do you face in being both distinct from and immersed in the lives of these 3 people?

7: Blessed are the merciful

Of all the endeavors I have undertaken, none has challenged me more than parenting our three children. It is not that they are needier than other children or that I lack affection or commitment toward them. No, the sole challenging factor is that they are mine. I bear responsibility for their lives. When my child has a need, I cannot respond, "That is not my problem." Any problem they have is my problem.

What about the other seven billion people in the world–those who are not my children, not my responsibility? That is where mercy comes in. Mercy looks at situations where you could say, "That is not my problem" and makes it your problem. We will look at a few stories from the Gospels that illustrate what mercy is and is not, but our starting place is the life of Jesus. In short, God could have looked at Adam and Eve's sinful rebellion and the death it brought into the world and said, "That is not my problem." But even in the delivery of punishment in the Garden of Eden, God spoke a word of mercy, a promise that one day this curse would be reversed. Because of his mercy, God the Father sent God the Son to enter into our sinful, death-ridden world until it killed him. Jesus made our problem of sin and death his problem, though it cost him his life. The world has never known greater mercy.

One of Jesus' most shocking illustrations of how we ought to likewise show mercy is the Good Samaritan (Luke 10:25-37), who used his time, transportation, money, and medical supplies to help a Jewish man that had been robbed, beaten, and left for dead. The sharp edge of the story is created by the word "Samaritan," as the ethnic animosity between Samaritans and Jews rivals that of any embattled groups today. Imagine a Palestinian coming across a nearly-dead Israeli in modern-day Jerusalem and you get the idea.

In Jesus' story, what marked the Samaritan as merciful began simply with direction. Whereas two religious leaders also walking the Jericho road "passed by on the other side" (Luke 10:31-32), the Samaritan "came to where [the beaten man] was." This was the entry point of mercy. Against every bitter instinct instilled in him, the Samaritan moved *toward* the bloodied Jewish man, "and when he saw him, he had compassion" (Luke 10:33).

Thus mercy begins with movement. The mercy Jesus blesses looks around and moves toward others with relational, emotional, financial, physical, and spiritual needs. Mercy asks others the simple question, "What do you need?" and asks God the question, "How would you have me deploy my resources to meet this person's needs?"

If we are honest, the call to move toward people in need makes us nervous. Perhaps we battle ethnic or class prejudice. Perhaps our time and money feels so scarce we cannot imagine sharing any. Perhaps an encounter would unveil insecurities in our lives. Perhaps we simply do not want to help others. These hesitations are real and they threaten to keep our lives very small.

When our hearts are revealed to lack mercy for others, Jesus' words should give us cause for concern. "Blessed are the merciful, for they shall receive mercy." We might think Jesus misspoke, since he consistently teaches elsewhere that God's mercy cannot be earned. But remember, Jesus is not commanding us to be merciful. He is blessing those who have encountered him in a way that has made them merciful. This chain reaction of mercy is so certain that Jesus can essentially say, "If my mercy toward you has not made you merciful toward others, then you have not really experienced my mercy and will not experience it when I return in judgment."

This is made explicit in Jesus' parable of the unforgiving servant in Matthew 18:23-35. The main character is a servant who owed a powerful king about $6 billion. Lest our minds go to Bill Gates, Warren Buffet, or any other modern figure who could pay such a debt, it should be clarified that this amount of money was more than existed in the entire known world. Jesus exaggerated to the point of absurdity, communicating the insurmountable size of the debt.

When the indebted servant begged the king for more time, the king, in a stunning display of mercy, relieved the debt entirely. However, when the forgiven servant left the palace, he hunted down a fellow servant who owed him $12,000. When this fellow servant made a familiar-sounding plea for more time, the man refused and threw him in prison until he repaid every last penny of this comparatively minuscule debt. The king, upon hearing this, threw the unforgiving servant in prison and demanded that he pay his original debt after all.

The point of Jesus' story is not that God will forgive me if I forgive others sufficiently. The point is that if I am told that I have been forgiven a $6 billion debt and go rough up a guy until he pays me $12,000, I have not really embraced my forgiveness of $6 billion. Thus when my heart equivocates about moving toward those in need around me, I must be reminded of the unfathomable mercy I have been shown by God. He owed me nothing, yet he gave me everything. Every morning I must pull out that statement of my $6 billion debt and weep over the words stamped across that bill: "Debt Forgiven." The first step of cultivating an ongoing posture of mercy is believing the gospel of mercy today.

From Jesus' own ministry and from these two stories we see what the merciful life looks like. It does not say, "That is not my problem" or deny to others what God has graciously given to us. Rather, mercy moves toward those in need to share freely. It is a display of God's gospel movement toward us.

Questions for reflection

❖Using your own words or the words above, how would you define mercy?

❖Who are the people (individuals or a certain type of person) whose needs you tend to walk away from? Why do you think their needs make you uncomfortable?

❖Do you think of your sin against God (moral debt) as a $6 billion, impossibly large debt or as something less drastic? What does this reveal about your need to embrace your poverty of spirit and mourn over your sin?

❖As you think about the the 3 people God has called you to minister to, what does it look like practically to move toward them mercifully?

Scriptures for deeper exploration

❖Biblical characters who knew themselves to be recipients of God's movement toward them:
  • Moses/Israel (Deuteronomy 7:6-21)
  • David (2 Samuel 7)
  • Paul (Ephesians 2:1-10, 1 Timothy 1:12-17)
❖Psalms meditating on or praying for God's mercy toward us:
  • Psalm 23
  • Psalm 28
  • Psalm 30
  • Psalm 51
  • Psalm 86
  • Psalm 123
❖Displays of mercy toward those in need:
  • God's bountiful mercy to four lepers (2 Kings 7)
  • David show mercy to Shimei (2 Samuel 16:5-14, 19:16-23)
  • Job's mercy to the poor (Job 29:7-20, 31:16-23)

When Jesus moved mercifully toward us, dying for our sins and rising to give us eternal life, he did so from a heart of obedience toward his Father and love for us. His motives were pure–unmixed, uncontaminated, singular, and genuine.

Regretfully the same is not always true of us. Our hearts are not always unified by love for God and neighbor. Ulterior motives creep into our interactions with others. We want something from them, like praise or recognition or gratitude. Perhaps impulses of lust or greed or resentment or pride begin to muddy the waters of our mercy. The purity of our motives is compromised.

Yet when we dwell with the broken, purity of heart is non-negotiable if we want them to see Jesus. This is most explicit in our Lord's teaching on being salt in a decaying world. He warned us in Matthew 5:13 not to let our salt lose its taste, its saltiness. Because salt does not naturally decay, the only way it could lose its effectiveness is by being mixed with sand or dirt. Likewise, when our desire for others to experience the blessings of Jesus' kingdom is compromised by our own self-focused desires, our ministry to them loses its potency. Our salt is "no longer good for anything except to be thrown out and trampled under people's feet" (Matthew 5:13).

In the remainder of the Sermon on the Mount, Jesus addresses two broad ways that our purity of heart could be contaminated. One is through our sinful inclinations. In Matthew 5 he tackles the heart issues of resentment (21-26), lust (27-30), duplicity (33-37), retaliation (38-42), and hatred of enemies (43-48). These are the undercover versions of the marquee sins of murder, adultery, lying, and revenge that hit the headlines when they take place in the church. But Jesus wants more than a scandal-free church; he wants sin-free hearts and thus exhorts us to take the internal versions of these sins as seriously as their external manifestations. He forces us to recognize that resentment is on the same spectrum as murder, lust is on the same spectrum as adultery, and duplicity is on the same spectrum as lying. The heart issues may not cause public outrage but, as Jesus' teaching on saltiness makes clear, they can compromise our effectiveness in bringing Jesus' news of redemption to fellow broken humans.

If we are in tune with the weaknesses of our hearts, this list of vices that threaten our saltiness will likely not surprise us. What may surprise us is Jesus' second category in which our hearts can be contaminated, namely, our "righteous deeds." In Matthew 6:1-18, Jesus shows how giving to the needy, prayer, and fasting can be hijacked by our lust for people's praise. In each case, he says, we get what we want when others applaud us for our deeds. Our good works are no longer bringing glory to our Father in heaven; they are bringing attention to us.

This is an insidious threat to our purity of heart, because it lies under the cloak of "doing good" to others. In the book of Acts the story is told of two families who sold property so they could share the proceeds with needy brothers and sisters in Christ. One was Barnabas, who "sold a field that belonged to him and brought the money and laid it at the apostles' feet" (Acts 4:37). The other was Ananias, who "sold a piece of property, and with his wife's knowledge he kept back for himself some of the proceeds and brought only a part of it and laid it at the apostles' feet" (Acts 5:1–2). From the outside, these two acts of generosity looked exactly the same. Yet Ananias' motives were mixed—one part generosity, one part greed, one part love of recognition.

What do we do when God exposes the impurity of our hearts, when our motives in ministry are revealed to be contaminated? Our temptation may be to retreat, to put our merciful movement toward the broken in reverse. In a few cases where obvious temptation abounds, this may be wise. But the only course of action that will address our real need is repentance. We must reengage in the process described in Jesus' first four blessings. We must allow God's Spirit to transform our spiritual poverty–through mourning and meekness–into hunger for right relationships with God and others. We must be broken all over again.

This may feel like defeat to us, as if we did not "get it" the first time and we can only hope repentance will "stick" this round. Yet this ongoing need for repentance simply reminds us of how deeply embedded sin is in our hearts. Our awareness of inner sinfulness will actually increase as we grow closer to God and move more mercifully toward broken people.

Thus we should not approach purity of heart as a perfected state of being that "super-Christians" achieve. Rather, purity of heart is a natural byproduct of the trajectory of brokenness, which leads to a single-minded hunger and thirst for God himself. Like those who engage in good works for applause, Jesus promises that those who are pure in heart will get what they want: they will see God. Only as our impure motives are replaced by righteous motives will we be salty, effective agents of change as we dwell with the broken.

Questions for reflection and Scriptures for deeper exploration

❖Read through the vices–both actions and sins of the heart–
Jesus catalogues in Matthew 5:21-48. Out of the list of
resentment (21-26), lust (27-30), duplicity (33-37), retaliation
(38-42), and hatred of enemies (43-48), which sins emerge the
most when you are ministering to others? Are there sins Jesus
does not mention in this passage that you struggle with while
ministering to others?

❖Read Jesus' teaching on how we should do our righteous
deeds in Matthew 6:1-18. Do you seek to make your good
works visible to others, in hopes of receiving their praise? If so,
how?

❖What emotions do you experience when you realize that even your ministry efforts are shot through with sinful intentions?

❖What next step do you need to take to pursue a pure heart?

9: Blessed are the peacemakers

One of the Hebrew words every follower of Jesus should know is "shalom." Though we translate it "peace," our English word is sorely inadequate for capturing the full meaning of shalom and, consequently, what it looks like to be a peacemaker. Shalom envelops much more than the absence of conflict; it describes an entire ecosystem of harmony, prosperity, safety, completion, and flourishing. We see shalom at the beginning of the Biblical story in the Garden of Eden. To even imagine what life in Eden was like we must envision various experiences: living in a nature preserve where the animals range free and do not bite, tending a fruitful garden with rich soil and limitless water, dining at an all-you-can-eat buffet with delicious and healthy food, worshiping God with unfettered joy, and being on an unending honeymoon with the love of your life. All of these experiences made up the fullness of shalom in Eden.

But when Adam and Eve rebelled against God, it affected shalom at every level of relationship: with God, with one another, with their self-understanding, and with the rest of creation. Adam and Eve fell from enjoying perfect shalom to hiding from God, turning on one another, feeling shame, and working thorny ground. God's curse because of their sin fractured shalom entirely. Things were no longer right in the world.

Peacemaking seeks the restoration of shalom on every level. It treats humans as whole beings who have spiritual, relational, identity, and physical needs, and it pursues human flourishing holistically. As with the other beatitudes, peacemaking is not a human initiative but a response to encountering Jesus. In particular, we labor toward restoring shalom because Jesus came as the ultimate peacemaker.

Think of the holistic nature of Jesus' ministry. The most obvious needs he met were physical–healing the lame man brought by four friends, feeding the 5,000, exorcising a demon from a little girl, raising Lazarus from the dead, and restoring a man's withered hand. The gospels are replete with stories of physical healing. Yet Jesus' ministry to the body often addressed some deeper need. Before healing the lame man, Jesus pronounced his sins forgiven, identifying his greater need of reconciliation with God (Mark 2:1-12). When the 5,000 who had been fed followed Jesus for more food, he pointed them to their spiritual need for God's true food, Jesus himself (John 6). When the woman with a demon-possessed little girl asked for help, Jesus pressed her on her sense of identity, as she hailed from a wealthy, oppressive class (Mark 7:24-30). The raising of Lazarus was physical proof that Jesus would indeed address our final need of resurrection life in his own resurrection (John 11:1-44). His Sabbath miracle of the man's withered hand intentionally challenged the spiritually abusive ways of the Pharisees (Mark 3:1-6, cf. Matt 23:13-36).

In each of these situations, Jesus' ministry to a person's physical need was legitimate in and of itself. It was not simply a "foot in the door," an excuse to get to a real need. The physical need was a real need. Yet the physical need was not the person's only need, just the most obvious. Underneath the hunger or withered hand was a relationship with God that needed to be restored, an unjust set of social relationships that needed to be addressed, a need for identity as God's image-bearer, or a fractured relationship of work and reward that needed renewal.

Here the call to dwell with people–to linger in their lives and walk with them through hardships–is made plain. Peacemaking is not a quick fix, like replacing a lightbulb. It is more like the renovation project that starts with the kitchen flooring then addresses the leaky pipes, inadequate wiring, and weak roof revealed by the original project. When we help our neighbor with grocery money, a heart for peacemaking could lead to anything from encouraging her to be reconciled with her sister to providing childcare while she attends job training to having a Bible study about God's love and forgiveness in Christ. All these seek to repair shalom where it has been fractured.

Put in these terms, we realize that we ourselves are still in the process of restoration. Our ongoing sin reveals the need for fresh reconciliation with God; we have unhealthy family relationships that require attention; our self-understanding does not match all that God says is true of us as his children; we have physical maladies; our work life is still filled with toil, sweat, and disappointment. These evidences of our own continuing need for grace and renewal should prevent us from presuming to be superheroes swooping in to fix the broken. Rather, we are the broken ones Jesus is making new and he sent us to invite others into the same restoration.

Final shalom–the completion of the renovation project–will not take place until Jesus returns in person to make all things finally and gloriously new. This has at least two very significant implications. First, it means we should not mistake our peacemaking efforts as the means by which God will ultimately change the world. This is by no means to downplay our involvement in others' experience of redemption. Rather, this identifies our ministry with Jesus' earthly ministry–one that gives hints and foretastes of the perfected kingdom he will bring about at his return. While we might not be the ultimate agents of change, our ministry of word (proclaiming the gospel of the kingdom) and deed (showing the peace that King Jesus brings) is God's chosen way to bring more and more broken sinners under his redemptive rule.

Second, this preserves us from despair when things are not getting better around us–when the unjust structure does not fall, when the estranged friends do not reconcile, or when the abuser goes unpunished. These do not represent a failure of God's kingdom, only a delay of his justice. Yet because Christ's return is sure, we labor with tenacity, undaunted by lost battles when his is the victory in war.

God's commitment to peace was displayed ultimately at the cross. He sent his own beloved Son to a cruel death so that we might have peace with God (Romans 5:1) and "to reconcile to himself all things, whether on earth or in heaven, making peace by the blood of his cross" (Colossians 1:20). As those who have received this peace through trust in Jesus, let us join God's peacemaking agenda with all that we have, looking to the final day when shalom will be our new, never-ending norm.

Questions for reflection

❖What is the Bible's definition of peace ("shalom" in Hebrew)?

❖As you think of the various components of shalom–spiritual, relational, identity (or psychological), and physical, which do you feel are in need of the most renovation in your life?

❖As you think about the 3 people God has called you to minister to, what are the most obvious needs for restoration in their lives? What deeper needs lie underneath those obvious needs?

❖The opportunity to be part of Jesus' peacemaking mission is an unparalleled privilege. What have you experienced in being in the middle of someone else's restoration of shalom?

❖God's restoration project does not always move as quickly as we would like. What are the areas of broken shalom–both personally and in others–that grieve you the most right now? Describe your emotional experience of these situations.

Scriptures for deeper exploration

❖God's concern for our holistic peace:
- Spiritual (Romans 5:1-11, Ephesians 2)
- Relational (Matthew 5:21-26, Romans 12:9-21, 2 Corinthians 13:11)
- Identity (1 Corinthians 6, Ephesians 1, Colossians 3:1-17)
- Physical (Matthew 25:31-46, 2 Corinthians 8, James 2:1-17, 1 John 3:11-18)

❖The final state of shalom after Jesus' return:
- Isaiah 65:17-25
- Revelation 21-22

10: Blessed are those who are persecuted for righteousness' sake

Consider this headline: "Angry Crowd Mobs Church for Feeding the Poor." Or this: "College Graduate Criticized for Joining Peace Corps." Or this: "Local Pastor Fired for Reconciling Marriages." Seem outrageous? They are. They are also fabricated. Yet the reality behind them is not, considering Jesus' blessing over those who are persecuted for laboring to make things right in the world. Why would he anticipate his fellow peacemakers to encounter maltreatment?

The answer begins with our assumptions about what is wrong in the world and, consequently, what must be done to make things right. For Jesus the problem boiled down to human sin and the remedy began with his call to "Repent, for the kingdom of heaven is at hand" (Matthew 4:17). There are billions in our world who do not agree with this conclusion and may find the Christian proclamation of repentance offensive. Furthermore, some of these stand to gain from the inequity and fractured relationships unrighteousness causes, motivating them to oppose acts of mercy and justice. Add God's prime enemy–Satan–into the equation and there will be conflict.

Historically, Christians have faced severe persecution for their faith. Indeed, today in much of the world, believers are martyred, land is confiscated, pastors are imprisoned, children are threatened, and church gatherings are dispersed by secret police. We may be less likely to suffer in these ways in America but we will face opposition. A friend in ministry recently shared his experience in a North American city where pulling out his copy of the Bible on a bus or in a coffee shop would attract antagonistic conversation. Even if this is not the case where we live, our very involvement in the lives of those under Satan's dominion will incur another form of persecution: spiritual attack, possibly in the form of physical illness, relational strife, or hurtful miscommunication. I have observed that our church comes under spiritual attack most when we step into the enemy's territory and address abusive relationships.

Regardless of the degree or nature of the persecution, the very possibility of opposition forces us to make a decision: do I love the pursuit of righteousness more than I love comfort? Persecution, at its core essence, robs us of one type of comfort or another–physical, emotional, spiritual, or relational. When these comforts are compromised, the fork in the road divides the path of staying on Jesus' agenda of making things right from the path of enjoying calm and ease in this life.

Church history abounds with inspiring stories of those who have chosen the path of pursuing righteousness over comfort. Two in particular strike me as indicative of the life Jesus blesses in Matthew 5:10–one a politician and one an educator. The first is William Wilberforce. Born in 1759, Wilberforce enjoyed such wealth and good connections in his native England that he ran for office at the age of 21 and won. Four years later, he encountered Jesus Christ in a way that would change him forever. During the next two years he wrestled with how to best engage in Jesus' agenda of righteousness and restoration of shalom. Then in 1787 he came into contact with a group fighting for the abolition of slavery and met the fork in the road. He could expend all his financial, political, and oratory capital on his own comfort or deploy it for the freeing of God's image-bearers who were being treated and traded as property. Wilberforce chose the latter road and dedicated his life to liberating oppressed slaves for 46 years. He died three days after learning that the Slavery Abolition Act was assured passage in Parliament.

A more contemporary and less well-known story is that of Dr. David Kasali. I met David in 2011, and his story has challenged me since. David hails from the Democratic Republic of Congo (DRC), a land torn by civil war and the brutal use of sexual violence to oppress entire villages. During the worst of the conflict, David started sensing God's call for him to move back to the DRC. He and his wife had earned doctorates in New Testament studies from a prestigious evangelical divinity school in the U.S. and he was enjoying a comfortable and thriving ministry as the President of a seminary in Nigeria. The fork in the road God began to reveal was, humanly speaking, a no-brainer. To return to the Congo would be suicidal. But this excuse only lasted so long, until God impressed on Dr. Kasali, "It's time to stop letting everyone else do the dying." Thus began David's journey home and the establishment of The Congo Initiative, which has a holistic vision of restoring this beautiful but devastated land. Because he loved righteousness more than comfort, David Kasali has opened the way for many in our church to be part of God's redemptive work in that country, which in turn has challenged our faith and action in our local context.

God calls different people to different areas of need. These two stories are meant to exemplify what it looks like to choose the path of pursuing justice and peace over the path of comfort. The path God puts in front of you may involve unborn children and their mothers who believe abortion is their only option. It could involve unhealthy families where the children need foster care and the parents need mentoring and support. It may be addressing the reality of sex trafficking and the needs of prostituted women for holistic healing. It could mean tutoring students in an economically and educationally disadvantaged neighborhood. Perhaps God has placed you in circles with CEOs or politicians or artists and is calling you to pursue the restoration of shalom in those circles. Or perhaps your days are filled with changing diapers, cleaning up spills, and breaking up squabbles amongst your children. Whatever path God puts in front of you, the question is the same: will I choose God's agenda of reconciling people to himself and to one another or will I avoid the messiness and brokenness around me and choose the path of most ease and comfort?

Questions for reflection

❖ Why would any follower of Jesus be persecuted for pursuing peace and seeking to make things right around them?

❖ Have you ever experienced persecution–whether from others or through spiritual attack–for your commitment to God's agenda of reconciliation? At the time, how did you view the opposition and the ministry you were doing (i.e., did it make you want to quit, did it embolden your work, etc.)?

❖What are the comforts you most enjoy and would most avoid relinquishing? How might your ministry to others compromise these comforts?

❖How can you nurture a deeper commitment to God's work of reconciliation that would sustain you when opposition comes?

Scriptures for deeper exploration

❖The history of the early church's persecution:
  • Acts 4:1-22, 5:12-42, 7:54-60, 12:1-5, 13-14, 16-28
❖How early church leaders responded to persecution:
  • 2 Corinthians 4, 11:16-12:10
  • Hebrews 10:32-39;
  • 1 Peter 1:3-9, 2:11-25, 3:8-4:19

Part III

Rejoice In Hope
Of Eternal Reward

11: Introduction

As we immerse ourselves in the lives of other broken people, one reality will become quickly evident: we are at war. Jesus stated pointedly, "The thief comes only to steal and kill and destroy. I came that they may have life and have it abundantly" (John 10:10). Our experience of dwelling with Jesus and dwelling with the broken lies in the crossfire of Satan's agenda of death and destruction and Jesus' agenda of life and renewal. As we saw in the teaching on persecution, we must expect that embracing Jesus' agenda will be costly.

What we need in the midst of this war is hope. When dark circumstances loom over our lives, we need to see the light that lies beyond the conflict, the promise of victory for those aligned with King Jesus. Hope can fuel endurance through the darkest seasons.

This dynamic is powerfully portrayed in a war scene from the final installment of Peter Jackson's *Lord of the Rings* films. Evil and exploitative armies have the upper hand over those that defend justice, peace, and beauty. One of the younger soldiers on the losing side, Pippin, hears the dark enemy pounding down one of the final gates and laments to his older mentor, "I didn't think it would end this way." Gandalf responds:

> "End? No, the journey doesn't end here. Death is just another path, one that we all must take. The grey rain-curtain of this world rolls back, and all turns to silver glass. And then you see it."
> "What, Gandalf? See what?"

"White shores...and beyond, a far green country under a swift sunrise."[6]

Pippin ponders this future for a bit then responds, "Well, that isn't so bad," which Gandalf knowingly echoes, "No. No, it isn't." The enemy breaks the gate down, their warriors pour through, and the battle resumes. Only now, Pippin fights with a new glint of hope.

Hope infuses Jesus' pronouncements of blessings over those who encounter him in repentance and trust. He promises comfort, satisfaction, and mercy. He guarantees the inheritance of the earth. He speaks of God's character being eternally visible in his children. And he pledges to his followers the greatest possible experience–they shall see God. All of these he pronounces over the ones who bow before him as King and embrace his agenda of righteousness.

Indeed, these expressions of hope are the very reason Jesus calls the repentant "blessed," signaled in each beatitude by the word "for." "Blessed are those who mourn, *for* they shall be comforted." "Blessed are the pure in heart, *for* they shall see God." The salt and light we offer to others is not ourselves but this magnificent blessing of hope that is captured in Jesus' promises. In our context of uncertainty–whether relational, financial, political, or physical–hope is a rare and precious commodity and our call to dwell with the broken is a call to deliver the message of hope.

Of course, we cannot fully share this blessing if we do not enjoy it ourselves. Thus the aim of this final set of meditations is

---

[6] *The Lord of the Rings: The Return of the King,* dir. Peter Jackson, New Line Cinema, 2003

to bask in the beautiful hope of Jesus' promises. If we dwell with Jesus until we are broken and dwell with the broken until they see Jesus, life will feel at times like a battle with little hope. Like Pippin, we will hear another injustice, another broken relationship, another need pounding down the gate and be tempted to say, "I didn't think it would end this way." In such moments of weariness and exhaustion we need hope. We need a break from the battle that takes in all the glory to come and bathes in it for a while.

As we walk through each of these promises (such as, "for they shall be comforted"), we will see that they are naturally connected to the heart posture associated with them ("Blessed are those who mourn"). That is, they are not arbitrary rewards like you might see on a game show, where guessing the price of laundry detergent is rewarded with a new car. Rather, they are natural rewards of a lifestyle, like enjoying the beauty of a flower one has nurtured. As C.S. Lewis put it, "The proper rewards are not simply tacked on to the activity for which they are given, but are the activity itself in consummation."[7]

This is only true because Jesus will return to bring his work of righteousness and peace to completion. He will make shalom an eternal reality on that final day. This alone is why the trajectory of brokenness ends in glory and why hope can be a real experience for us now. The heart that mourns over sin now will be comforted when Jesus rids the world of sin. The heart that hungers and thirsts for things to be made right will be finally satisfied when Jesus does just that. The heart with a singular desire to see God will indeed see him on that final day.

With such an end to our current posture of brokenness, we have every reason to experience great joy amidst deep sorrow. This was our Lord's journey through the cross to the resurrection and such will be ours as we hold fast to him. As you pause, reflect on Jesus' promises, and use your imagination regarding

---

[7] C.S. Lewis, *The Weight of Glory,* p. 4

the good things to come, may these brief meditations provide relief and renewal for the battle. May they strengthen your soul so that you may press on with hope.

Questions for reflection

❖Of all the glorious realities Jesus will bring about at his return, which ones give you the most hope in the present? Which ones are the most difficult to believe?

❖How do those promises affect your experience of sin, sorrow, and death in this present age?

❖ Describe a situation where you experienced joy in the midst of sorrowful circumstances.

12: Theirs is the kingdom of heaven

What separates hope from wishful thinking? How can we have reasonable confidence that something will actually happen in the future? To be more specific, what assurance do we have that Jesus will make good on his promises of eternal comfort, land, and pleasure?

This first promise–"Blessed are the poor in spirit, for theirs is the kingdom of heaven"–reminds us that the kingdom Jesus proclaimed was not merely pie in the sky when you die. The "kingdom" is synonymous with the reign or authority or dominion of a king, and Jesus' kingdom was both a present reality and a promise of things to come. It was present in his authoritative acts of healing and exorcism yet Jesus preached that the kingdom's fullness will be realized in the future. In food terms, the impressive appetizer assures us of an extraordinary entrée. This is why the beatitudes pledge present belonging in the kingdom ("theirs *is* the kingdom of heaven" [Matthew 5:3, 10]) while offering most of the kingdom's blessings as coming promises ("for they *shall...*" [Matthew 5:4-9]).

If we are acquainted with enough of the sorrows of this life, we will inevitably question whether an eternity of flourishing and joy is a pipe dream. Thus our hope of forever paradise must remain grounded in the one who came handing out samples of paradise. Jesus cast out demons, restored sight to the blind, retrieved a beloved daughter from death's grasp, and told a paralytic that his sins were as forgiven as his legs were healed. These were not party tricks to garner a following; they were pinholes in the night sky, allowing thin beams of eternal glory into the domain of Satan and sin and death. Jesus' mighty deeds assure us that, once he peels back death's veil for good, his full reign will shine like the sun forever. Hope is no fool's whim, no wishful thinking. It is grounded in reality just as the cross where

Jesus bore our death was fixed in the dirt of Calvary and his tomb vacated three days later.

The legitimacy of hope owes not only to Jesus' work for us 2,000 years ago but also to his work in us today. The Bible uses the language of "new creation" to describe the final state that God will bring about with the full exercise of his authority. But new creation is not on hold until Jesus' return. New creation is the present experience of everyone who is united to Jesus by faith (2 Corinthians 5:17). Our experience of being "born again" now is proof that Jesus will bring new, eternal life to the whole creation.

In particular, this experience of new creation is made real in us by the Holy Spirit. Jesus equated being born again with being born of the Spirit (John 3:5-8). The new birth is an example of the Spirit's ministry of granting us present tastes of the future fullness of Jesus' kingdom. The apostle Paul captures this dynamic of present and future by calling the Spirit the down payment or "guarantee of our inheritance until we acquire possession of it" (Ephesians 1:14). He also refers to the Spirit as the "firstfruits" of our final redemption (Romans 8:23). With both metaphors, a fraction is given presently to guarantee that the full amount will be coming. The briefcase with $10,000 cash ensures the $10,000,000 inheritance. The few sheaves of wheat are the firstfruits of 40 acres of harvest.

The Spirit's present work in your life can assure you that Jesus will make good on his promises spelled out in the beatitudes. When the Spirit enlivens your heart to adore God's splendor, love a spiteful coworker, break out of sinful patterns, or taste God's faithful love for you, these are confidence-building down payments and firstfruits of a world of good to come. They give you every reason to hope in the new creation of all things that Jesus will realize at his return.

As you reflect on the "for they shall..." promises in the days to come, ask the Holy Spirit to grant you tastes of the glory of Jesus' future kingdom. Pray for assurances that will encourage, embolden, and invigorate your soul for present faithfulness until the return of our King.

Questions for reflection

❖Jesus' promises of reward in Matthew 5:3-12 are staggering, though our hearts may struggle to feel this. Describe the hesitations you have in believing that he will actually give you these tremendous blessings.

❖As you read the gospels, do Jesus' mighty deeds bolster your belief that he will bring about his promises? Does the Spirit's present work in your life give you assurance for the future? What other meditations about what God has already done help you believe in what he has promised to do?

13: They shall be comforted

The hope of comfort is the assurance of release from all that grieves us in this life. We are often burdened by the weight of our own sin, of broken relationships, of failing bodies, of unjust social structures, of generational poverty, of war, of famine, and of the exploitation of the weak. As we saw earlier in our study, we often cope with these realities through distraction or succumb to despair. But Jesus promises that we who choose to mourn over the sin within and around us will be comforted.

This is nearly unimaginable to us when brokenness is inescapable in our world. Yet as much as we must strain our hearts to envision such a place, King Jesus guarantees a perfected kingdom in which no cause for mourning will remain. The apostle John saw a vision of this brilliant future when God showed him the New Heavens and New Earth. "And I heard a loud voice from the throne saying, 'Behold, the dwelling place of God is with man. He will dwell with them, and they will be his people, and God himself will be with them as their God. He will wipe away every tear from their eyes, and death shall be no more, neither shall there be mourning, nor crying, nor pain anymore, for the former things have passed away'" (Revelation 21:3-4).

The closest we get to this type of experience in our world is a weekly Sabbath or an occasional vacation. These opportunities to get away from the chaos around us are gifts, necessary times to refresh ourselves from seasons of engaging a fallen world. But in the back of our minds—even on the beach or in the mountains or in the quiet place of rest—we know that we must return to a world in which injustice reigns, the weak suffer, and God is not honored by his creation.

The beauty of comfort in the new creation is that no such "back of the mind" exists. There will be no sorrowful situation that we must ignore for the sake of refreshment. Imagine waking up in this new reality. Your body is like Jesus' resurrected body, not a hint of ache or pain. Your relationships are pure–no misunderstandings, no ulterior motives, no miscommunication. The community you live in shares a common value for the glory of God and love for one another. Food abounds and all delight in sharing their wealth. Abuse, exploitation, violence, hatred, and loss are but faint memories of a long-past era. No reason for mourning remains. Not only this, you live in perfect fellowship with the One who has wiped away every tear from your eyes, the God of all comfort who feeds you from the tree of life whose leaves are "for the healing of the nations" (Revelation 22:2).

This is the promise Jesus sets forth for those who mourn over the current state of affairs. Apart from this hope, the call to mourn would only yield burnout. But with this future of glory, we can weep well in the present as we look to the perfected kingdom Jesus will bring about and know that comfort will be our new reality.

Questions for reflection

❖Identify the issue that brings you the most grief presently. Now imagine that issue completely resolved by Jesus' powerful intervention. Pause over this and describe what comfort feels like.

❖How could the prospect of an eternity of comfort enable you to engage present realities with mourning instead of ignoring or despairing over them?

14: They shall inherit the earth

We can become so used to the metaphors of Jesus' teachings (cutting off one's right hand, a camel entering through the eye of a needle, etc.) that we fail to take him literally when we ought. So to be plain, when Jesus says that the meek are blessed because they will inherit the earth, there is no hidden, spiritual meaning underneath that promise. He actually means that we will inherit the earth.

Think of the first people that inherited the earth. After God created a beautiful, habitable, and good earth, he told Adam and Eve, "Behold, I have given you every plant yielding seed that is on the face of all the earth, and every tree with seed in its fruit. You shall have them for food" (Genesis 1:29). The Garden of Eden was a gift our first parents inherited. Likewise, when God told the children of Abraham about the Promised Land, he described it as having "great and good cities that you did not build, and houses full of all good things that you did not fill, and cisterns that you did not dig, and vineyards and olive trees that you did not plant" (Deuteronomy 6:10–11). In both cases God's people inherited a good, sustainable land that he entrusted into their stewardship, commanding them to cultivate and enjoy it.

What will the land Jesus promises be like? The book of Revelation brims with tantalizing impressions of its brilliance and beauty. The new creation will have garden-like features: a life-giving river that flows from God's throne and the tree of life that yields nourishing fruit and healing leaves (Revelation 22:2). Yet the new creation is not a garden but a city. The new Jerusalem has "the glory of God, its radiance like a most rare jewel, like a jasper, clear as crystal" (Revelation 21:11). "The city was pure gold," "the foundations of the wall of the city were adorned with every kind of jewel," and "each of the gates [was] made of a single pearl" (Revelation 21:18, 19, 21).

This description, plus our culture's general impressions about heaven, might lead us to think that the new Jerusalem is the ultimate retirement community, a place of eternal vacation. But the broader context of Revelation suggests that it is rather a place of eternal *vocation*, a place to joyfully steward and cultivate just as Adam and Eve in Eden and Israel in the Promised Land. One author explains,

> The New Jerusalem is more than paradise regained. As a city it fulfills humanity's desire to build out of nature a human place of human culture and community. True, it is given by God and so comes down from heaven. But this does not mean humanity makes no contribution to it. It consummates human history and culture insofar as these have been dedicated to God (Revelation 21:12, 14, 24, 26), while excluding the distortions of history and culture into opposition to God that Babylon represents (21:8, 27; 22:15)... The city that both includes paradise unspoiled (22:1-2) and is adorned with the beauty of paradise (21:19) points to that harmony of nature and human culture to which ancient cities once aspired but which modern cities have increasingly betrayed.[8]

Jesus promises a land that will provide endless enjoyment and purpose as a place to explore, marvel, and work. The labor will not be with sweat and thorns, but with satisfaction and bounty. The new creation, like the original, will be very good.

In our day as we await this inheritance, it is typically the wealthy that own the best land and, in many countries, this is attained through corruption and oppression. But in the age to come, the forever era when Jesus is King, land will not be

---

[8] Richard Bauckham, *The Theology of the Book of Revelation*, p. 135

bought or sold or stolen or confiscated. Land will be inherited. King Jesus will apportion land, not to the privileged and powerful, but to the meek–those who submit to God's agenda rather than forcing their own. This will leave us no room to be smug with entitlement. The farms and fields, mountains and lakes, beaches and caves will be ours by grace. This coming inheritance should set us free from the drive to possess more and more in this brief life. We will see others scrape and claw for their piece of earth but we can rest easy, knowing that one day all will be ours.

Questions for reflection

❖How have you envisioned Heaven in the past? How is this different from the Bible's descriptions of the New Heavens and New Earth?

❖ What aspects of life in a perfected physical creation excites you the most (i.e., exploring, farming, building, artistry, etc.)? What can you imagine yourself doing?

❖ How could such meditations affect your present work and attitude toward possessions?

15: They shall be satisfied

Satisfaction is the ice-cold drink after mowing the lawn, the team celebration after winning the tournament, the bonus check after a stretch of hard work, the nourishing meal after a taxing day of labor. Satisfaction is the gratifying consummation of labor and expectation. Thus to appreciate Jesus' promise of eternal satisfaction, we must pause to appreciate what will be satisfied at his return–the hunger and thirst for righteousness.

As we have already observed, righteousness involves right relationships with God and others. Thus craving for righteousness moves us into God's work of pursuing spiritual and social reconciliation, that is, peacemaking with God and others. Consider first the social component. This is well-known to us since the hunger and thirst for human equity often drives the stories on our screens, stages, and pages. The drama is created by the unjust antagonist: the abusive husband, the emotionally manipulative mother (or, more often, stepmother), the corrupt politician, the greedy corporate fat cat, or the ruthless military leader. The first act establishes the tyrannical rule of this "big bad," the second act chronicles the hero or people's fight for justice, and the final act–where satisfaction comes into the picture–shows the demise of the oppressor and the freedom of the oppressed.

Such is the hope that Jesus promises when he proclaims, "Blessed are those who hunger and thirst for righteousness, for they shall be satisfied" (Matthew 5:6). When God makes all things new, he will banish "the cowardly, the faithless, the detestable...murderers, the sexually immoral, sorcerers, idolaters, and all liars" (Revelation 21:8) from his restored creation. Their eternal destiny will be the lake of fire while the people of God will dwell with him in perfect communion. The celebration of justice in the third act will echo forward throughout eternity.

Pause for a moment to allow this good news to wash over you. In the kingdom Jesus is bringing, not a trace of unrighteousness will remain. Watchdog groups and activist movements will be rendered obsolete because there will be no story to expose, no exploitation to uncover, and no oppression to decry. Those desires in all of us for human relationships to be whole and healthy and life-giving will be finally and forever satisfied.

Now consider the part of the story our culture does not tell–that of our need for spiritual reconciliation, peace with God. As long as one ounce of rebellion toward God resides in our hearts, a world of harmony will never exist. The root of all these social injustices is our sinful posture against God. This is why educational development, charitable initiatives, economic stimulation, and diplomatic efforts–for all the short-term good they can do–will never suffice to bring about lasting change. Only the eradication of sin from human hearts will make change last and this is exactly what Jesus promises for those who trust in him.

Ultimate satisfaction will come when we find ourselves in renewed bodies with renewed hearts that beat only for the glory of God. No more will we be tempted to worship pleasure, power, or comfort more than our Creator. No more will we question whether the great I AM can be trusted. No more will we attempt to rule our lives rather than submitting to the Sovereign Lord. Jesus' death for us will have purged every trace of rebellion, unbelief, and disobedience from our hearts. We will be so perfectly centered on the glory of God that our natural instinct will be to worship, trust, and obey him alone. We will forever taste the freedom of uninhibited intimacy with Father, Son, and Holy Spirit.

This alone will create a society of justice in which there will be no poor, weak, or oppressed. Locks on doors, insurance for wealth, vaults for treasures, and contracts for agreements will be unnecessary. Our restored communion with God will translate into perfect communion with one another. As we adore our King's splendor and cultivate his new creation, each will get his due from the land and will enjoy the abundance of that perfected place. We will collaborate on work projects, share the land's valuable resources, and create artistic expressions that tell the story of God's redemption and grace. Harmony will be restored and we will rest, fulfilled in the joy of life as it was meant to be.

As we hunger and thirst for that righteousness to become reality, may we immerse ourselves in the lives of those who need reconciliation with God and others, pointing them to the hope that Jesus makes possible.

Questions for reflection

❖Describe the satisfaction you have experienced when an issue of injustice that burdened you was resolved for the good.

❖Imagine that taste of satisfaction being the norm in the new creation. What words describe that future reality?

16: They shall receive mercy

Earlier we used the Good Samaritan story to explore what it looks like to show mercy. Now imagine yourself as the man beaten and left for dead to taste what it means to receive mercy. You are semi-conscious, immersed in pain, and struggling to breathe. Between the beating and the bright sun you can only manage to crack open your eyes and you see a man approaching you, wearing priestly clothes. You do not have the strength even to call out for help so your only hope is if he moves toward you. He does not. In fact, he moves away from you, passing by on the other side of the road. A few minutes later the scene repeats itself, this time with a different priest. As he crosses to the other side of the road, you despair that any help will come since two religious leaders passed you by.

The next time you regain consciousness, you see another person approaching you. As you make out the figure you realize that, not only is he not a priest, he is not even Jewish. He is a Samaritan, though you typically use other, less kind names for those people. You think of all the things you would do to a helpless Samaritan and reach for any strength you can muster to escape his next move. You have nothing, so you are left for him to unleash whatever ethnic anger he wishes on you. As you prepare for the worst, you feel a wet cloth wiping the dirt and blood off of your face. You feel oil and wine poured over your wounds, then bandages binding them. Then your entire body is in the arms of this man who you assumed meant you harm. He places you on his donkey and takes you to the nearest inn, leaving sufficient payment for your healing and rest and promising to cover any further expenses.

Mercy is the distance between what a person deserves and what that person receives. This is a distance we can measure intellectually, but ultimately it is something we experience, just as the man left for dead tasted a depth of inexplicable, undeserved kindness and compassion from the Samaritan.

The Apostle Paul measures the distance between what we deserve before God and what we receive from him in Ephesians 2. Unlike the bit of life left in the man robbed and beaten on the Jericho road, we were "dead in trespasses and sins" (Ephesians 2:1)—not physically inactive and lifeless, but spiritually dead, such that we "lived in the passions of our flesh, carrying out the desires of the body and the mind" (2:3). What did this lifestyle deserve? Judgment. Eternal punishment. We "were by nature children of wrath, like the rest of mankind" (2:3).

Though this is what we deserved, what did we receive in Christ? God made us alive, raised us up, and "seated us with him in the heavenly places in Christ Jesus" (2:5-6). Like the Good Samaritan, God moved toward us in our helplessness and addressed our deepest needs. And why did he do this? What explains this immense gap between the hell we deserve and the heaven we have been given? God is "rich in mercy" and acts "because of the great love with which he loved us" (2:4).

When Jesus promises that the merciful "shall receive mercy" (Matthew 5:7), he certainly references the final judgment in which we will be welcomed into heaven rather than cast into hell. In that courtroom, despite all of the counts against us of hatred, resentment, greed, lust, pride, and a thousand other infractions of God's law, we will be declared "righteous" because of Christ's death and resurrection for us (cf. Romans 3:21-26, 4:22-25). The scene will doubtless leave us awe-struck, as those who committed the same sins as us but did not trust in Christ for salvation will be judged according to their works and thrown into the lake of fire. While we enter eternal life, they will taste the second death (Revelation 20:11-15). The merciful distance between what we deserve and what we receive will be palpable.

Yet this promise of mercy will not end at the judgment. The end-times ruling by the divine Judge in Revelation 20 will open up a new world to his people–the New Heavens and New Earth of Revelation 21 and 22. We will dwell with God in a world free of death, sorrow, and pain. We will drink from the spring of the water of life. We will marvel at the bejeweled brilliance of the New Jerusalem. We will bask in the light of the glory of God. We will enjoy the best of human cultivation in the perfected world. We will eat from the tree of life and experience its healing power. We will see the face of God and worship him forever. All of these will fill out the "what we receive" paradise that is separated by infinite mercy from the "what we deserve" lake of fire. Awe at the mercy of God will permeate our eternal experience.

Such is our hope as we navigate a world filled with neglect, bitterness, resentment, and revenge. Even our efforts to display mercy will be met with ingratitude, rejection, and attack. May our drive to dwell with the broken until they see Jesus be fueled by our present tastes of Christ's mercy and an eager anticipation of the infinite mercy to come.

Questions for reflection

❖What did you feel as you imagined yourself as the man helped by the Good Samaritan? Does this approximate how you view Jesus saving you?

❖How can you nurture an experience of Christ's mercy in a way that will sustain you in a world with little mercy?

17: They shall see God

The soundtrack of the Grand Canyon affirms one basic truth about humans: we desire to see glory. By soundtrack I mean the variety of languages being spoken as crowds press against the rails of the lookouts along the South Rim. The mix of German, Japanese, French, Spanish, Russian, and a dozen other languages testifies to the awe, the wonderment, the reverence we yearn to experience. This explains the great efforts we make to savor natural beauty, fine art, cinematic spectacle, and stunning architecture.

As magnificent as these sights may be, their splendor is but a flicker compared to the sun of God's uncreated glory. When Moses made the bold request, "Please show me your glory" (Exodus 33:18), the divine response was ultimately, "you cannot see my face, for man shall not see me and live" (Exodus 33:20). Instead, God hid Moses in a rock and allowed him to see his back after he had passed by. The very dust his splendor kicked up was enough to radiate Moses' face to intimidating proportions.

In view of this, Jesus' promise in Matthew 5:8 that the pure in heart "shall see God" ranks among his most astonishing teachings. No rocks, no hiding, no veil, no filter. They shall see God. The broader teaching of the New Testament informs us that such a vision will only be possible when our bodies are resurrected like Jesus', our eyes finally capable of seeing God and living to tell the story. My guess is that once we have seen this glory, we will not want to take our eyes off of him.

In John's vision of the New Jerusalem, our forever home with God, he noted that "I saw no temple in the city, for its temple is the Lord God the Almighty and the Lamb. And the city has no need of sun or moon to shine on it, for the glory of God gives it light, and its lamp is the Lamb" (Revelation 21:22–23). In short, the resplendence of God will permeate the entire new creation. We will open our eyes after a nap and see the glory of God. We will look out the window of our home and behold divine beauty. The most spectacular vision our redeemed eyes could ever behold will be what we will constantly behold, world without end.

This is the promise to those who are pure in heart. Ours is a world that caters to all manner of impurities of the heart, downplaying the glory of God and exalting the glory of sex, money, and power. These are empty promises, yet they have real power to sully our communion with God and derail our mission to others. In the face of such temptation, it is our meditation on our destiny of seeing God forever that can empower present single-hearted affections for God. For "we know that when [Jesus] appears we shall be like him, because we shall see him as he is. And everyone who thus hopes in him purifies himself as he is pure" (1 John 3:2–3).

Questions for reflection

❖Describe an encounter in which you have been stunned by beholding the splendor of God (or, if you have not experienced this, some other encounter with beauty).

❖Imagine an eternity in which you behold infinitely greater magnificence at all times. How could dwelling on this destiny empower you to avoid fixating on lesser (and perhaps sinful) glories in this life?

18: They shall be called sons of God

"You remind me a lot of your dad."

I remember everything about the evening when a friend spoke those words to me–the old wooden chapel, the lump in my 13 year-old throat before I spoke, the crowd of more than 75 peers at our church camp, and the words I said during the post-service share time. That summer evening is fixed in my mind because of the sense of identity those words granted me. I respected my dad more than anyone on the planet, and now my friend was blessing me by pinpointing a family resemblance. (This experience may not resonate with you, but imagine hearing "You remind me a lot of..." and fill in the blank with someone you highly respect.)

There is a sense in which all who trust in Jesus are God's children through our adoption into God's family. But Jesus' promise of being identified as sons of God captures a different dynamic, namely that when we pursue the restoration of peace in our world we bear the character of our Father in heaven. He initiated reconciliation at the cost of his own Son, and when we adopt his agenda of peace, others can identify, "You remind me a lot of your Father."

Is this a promise only for males? Will sisters in Christ be called "sons" of God? The reason for the language is due to the way the label "son of" was used in biblical times. While it could denote family relationships, it could also be used to identify character, like Paul's pronouncement against an enemy of the gospel–"You son of the devil, you enemy of all righteousness, full of all deceit and villainy" (Acts 13:10). The apostle was not identifying a father-son relationship but a character resemblance between the devil and this opponent of Jesus.

Thus all who engage in God's peacemaking activity in the world will forever taste the pleasure of being identified with the character of our heavenly Father. This reflection of God's attributes is a restoration of our original identity and vocation as his image-bearers. This should give hope to all of us, but especially to those who have endured various forms of abuse that communicated a twisted sense of identity. Those harmful, deep-seated lies will be absent in God's good world. Because of the work the Father has done in us through his crucified and risen Son and the transformation of the Spirit, will forever bask in the joy of belonging to and resembling the divine family.

Questions for reflection

❖What voices or experiences have given you an unhealthy sense of identity? Describe what it will feel like to live in a perfected community where such lies will not exist.

❖In the new creation we will both be God-centered and have a healthy sense of identity. How will this be different from your current experience of receiving praise and giving God praise?

19: Rejoice and be glad!

I have yet to meet a happily married person who pines for the days of engagement. Truth be told, engagement is a necessary but frustrating season. Preparations for the wedding and life together require this time, but it is characterized by unfulfilled desire and separation. When Rachael and I were engaged, my saddest moments occurred on the drive back to my apartment after dropping her off at hers. How could I be "going home" when I felt most at home with my fiancé? The only thing that cheered that miserable trip was the thought that one day soon there would be no separation, no boundaries, no unconsummated desire. On that day we would remain home together.

Our meditations in this part of the study have focused on future realities–comfort and satisfaction, inheriting the earth, tasting mercy, seeing God, and being identified with our Father. To use the wedding analogy (as Revelation 19 does), the full experience of these benefits comes after the wedding, after the marriage supper of the Lamb. Now we find ourselves in a period much like engagement, where we are in a covenant relationship with God yet are not tasting the fullness of this relationship. Little wonder that the Apostle Paul writes that we "groan inwardly as we wait eagerly" (Romans 8:23) for the consummation of our deliverance from this world into God's perfected creation.

Yet groaning and waiting are not the only experiences of this premarital season. Like my smile-inducing musings as I drove away from Rachael's apartment, we have every reason for tasting present joy as we meditate on the fullness of Christ's kingdom. This has been the aim of contemplating Jesus' promises as we have, that we might experience a foretaste of the good things to come. Thus Jesus commands us, "Rejoice and be glad, for your reward is great in heaven, for so they persecuted the prophets who were before you" (Matthew 5:12). Our anticipation of future, heavenly reward can create real joy and gladness now.

Jesus means for this joy to fuel our endurance through persecution. His command to "Rejoice and be glad" comes on the coattails of his pronouncement, "Blessed are those who are persecuted for righteousness' sake" (Matthew 5:10), and its expanded version in verse 11–"Blessed are you when others revile you and persecute you and utter all kinds of evil against you falsely on my account" (Matthew 5:11). Such persecuted folk are blessed because, like the prophets of old, their persecution identifies them as being on the winning team, the right side of history. The two millennia since Jesus' words are permeated with stories of persecuted, reviled, falsely accused brothers and sisters who now taste the fullness of their heavenly reward. Jesus calls us to join their ranks. And he does so, not as one unscathed by injury, but the one "who for the joy that was set before him endured the cross, despising the shame, and is seated at the right hand of the throne of God" (Hebrews 12:2).

As we finish this study of the beatitudes, may the message ringing in your ears be Jesus' call to hope, joy, and gladness. As you continue on the trajectory of brokenness and remain immersed in the lives of broken people, may the most pressing priority of your heart be to taste now–by the Spirit's power–the delight of our eternal home with God. This may seem contradictory to the call to dwell with the broken if you have been raised with the fear of being "so heavenly minded that you are no earthly good." I leave you with the words of C.S. Lewis to combat this misconception, in hopes that you will join the ranks of those who have been potent salt and light in ages past.

> If you read history you will find that the Christians who did most for the present world were precisely those who thought most of the next. The Apostles themselves, who set on foot the conversion of the

Roman Empire, the great men who built up the Middle Ages, the English Evangelicals who abolished the Slave Trade, all left their mark on Earth, precisely because their minds were occupied with Heaven. It is since Christians have largely ceased to think of the other world that they have become so ineffective in this.[9]

May you do much for this present world as you dwell with Jesus and others in the hope of eternal reward.

Questions for reflection

❖Look over the promises of Matthew 5:3-12. Describe a few joy-filled tastes of these promised rewards that the Spirit has given you.

---

[9] C.S. Lewis, *Mere Christianity*, p. 104

❖Write a prayer acknowledging the promises that are most difficult for you to embrace now. Ask the Spirit to give you experiences of these promises and, in that, joyful endurance through present trials.

Guide for Leaders

Addressing broken and messy lives is always done best with others who desire to experience God's redemptive power in and around them. Thus this devotional would be most effectively experienced in a one-on-one setting or a small group (3-5) of brothers or sisters. The dynamics of any group will be as different as the answers to questions throughout the devotional, so no cookie cutter how-to is possible. But here are some suggestions for meeting with others and leading them through this experience of the beatitudes.

Expectations

In speaking with others about the possibility of meeting together, be clear about your expectations of their involvement in the group. They should commit to:

❖ Attend each meeting, barring sickness or being out of town.

❖ Read each section and work through the questions each week (requires at least 30 minutes of uninterrupted time 2-3 times per week).

❖ Be willing to share the existence of doubts or struggles, even if the person is not comfortable with sharing the particulars about those doubts or struggles.

❖ Prayerfully consider working through this devotional with others as God leads them.

Hopefully these points communicate a particular feel that the groups should have. This is not a Bible study where the transfer of information is the primary goal. The aim of this devotional is the transformation of our lives as we encounter our glorious God, take honest stock of our own lives, and make ourselves available to engage hurting people around us. The sharing should be real but appropriate. When one member takes a risk and shares something personal, the response of the others in the group should be empathetic and encouraging without stopping to "fix" a situation or to preach to that person until he or she sees things differently. The group should be a place where you as a leader can model what it means to "dwell with the broken until they see Jesus."

This process of grappling with Jesus' teaching is, categorically, discipleship. As a leader you are "teaching them to observe all that I have commanded you" (Matthew 28:20). This is why you want to encourage each person in your group, from the beginning, to prayerfully consider who God might call them to serve by exploring these issues of brokenness and ministry together.

Schedule

While the readings are intentionally not extensive (depending on how much of the "Scriptures for deeper exploration" the members read), they hit deep issues in our lives. Thus the length of the study may be dictated by how deeply the members in your group are wrestling with the topics raised. With that being said, the group will likely meet for a period of 8-12 weeks. Here is a possible schedule for meeting for 8 weeks:

Week 1	Read Introduction*
Week 2	1-3
Week 3	4-5
Week 4	6-8
Week 5	9-10
Week 6	11-13
Week 7	14-16
Week 8	17-19

*The first meeting is primarily a time for each member to share a 10-minute version of their life story—what type of spiritual environment they grew up in, how they came to trust in Christ, the events and relationships that have shaped them the most, etc.–as well as a time for you to set the tone for the group by reiterating the expectations above. Then you can read the introduction to the Dwell devotional out loud and have a few minutes of discussion about brokenness and how familiar or unfamiliar the group members are with the concept.

Discussion

As the leader of the group, your role is to guide the discussion time. This requires wisdom and attention. You want everyone to have an opportunity for input, which requires discretely bringing the sharing of some to a close while asking others to share, hopefully without embarrassing either one. If you are naturally talkative, you may need to force yourself to allow for an uncomfortable amount of silence after asking a question until someone shares. Remember, you are not a lecturer but a discussion facilitator.

If you go by the schedule above, you will have 2-3 sections to cover in each meeting and it will work best to cover the sections one at a time. As you read each section in your own preparation time, write down any questions that come to mind for the group and take note of which questions are more personal than others. When you begin discussing the section in the meeting, start by asking someone to explain the general concept of that section (poor in spirit, mercy, pure in heart, etc.). This may seem like stating the obvious but it is key for making sure everyone is on the same page. Then open the floor for anyone to share what stood out to them most from the reading. This may elicit no response or it could consume the bulk of your time. Once everyone has had an opportunity to share, begin asking questions from the devotional and the questions you wrote down. This is where wisdom will be required based on how well you know your group. If the brothers or sisters do not know each other very well, begin with the less personal questions and see where the conversation goes. It may take a few weeks before the group is ready for the more personal questions, or things could move in that direction in the first meeting. Obviously no one has to answer any question but it is still good to have a game plan regarding which questions to ask based on the level of familiarity and transparency in the group. Your own transparency in sharing will help move the group forward.

May God bless you as you pray for those in your group, prepare for each meeting, and pursue brokenness and renewal with your friends in Christ!